To Provide All People

Owen Sheers

ff

FABER & FABER

First published in 2018
by Faber & Faber Limited
Bloomsbury House
74–77 Great Russell Street
London WC1B 3DA
This paperback edition published in 2019

Typeset by Faber & Faber Limited
Printed and bound by CPI Group (UK) Ltd, Croydon, CR0 4YY

The right of Owen Sheers to be identified as author of this work
has been asserted in accordance with Section 77 of the Copyright,
Designs and Patents Act 1988

*To be published alongside the Vox Pictures/BBC Cymru Wales production
broadcast to mark the occasion*

BBC logo © BBC 2017
BBC and the BBC logo are trademarks of the British Broadcasting Corporation
and are used under licence

A CIP record for this book
is available from the British Library

ISBN 978–0–571–34808–4

2 4 6 8 10 9 7 5 3 1

To Siriol
and all who've helped her be here

Contents

*HYWEL, a porter, watches the dawn from
a third-floor window
in Nevill Hall hospital, Abergavenny.
An empty bed stands beside him.*

Hywel

Here's a thing.
How, exactly, would you say
does an idea begin? Where does it all start?
In one woman's brain? One man's heart?
Doesn't seem likely, does it?

I mean, all of us are fuelled
by the thoughts of others,
by what we've read, gleaned or seen.
Take all this – health care, medicine,
didn't just rise from nowhere, did it?

Someone, somewhere, I always think,
back across the millennia, must have been the first –
to lay a hand on the wound of a stranger.
In a cave maybe, ice at its mouth,
a fire beside. Or perhaps later, in a hut or a shelter.

Wherever, whenever it was,
someone must have been the first –

to offer comfort beyond their tribe
not because they had to or should,
but because they could.

> *He takes up the empty bed*
> *and pushes it on down the corridor.*

Someone else again would have seen that,
watched, learnt how to do the same –
what staunched the blood, eased the pain.
And so it must have begun within us,
not so much an idea as an offering –

a caring chain of practice and knowledge;
a refusal as a species to just lie down and take it
but rather, through attention,
intelligence, care, foster a belief
in our agency in life –

our ability to pit our empathy and wit
against sickness, disease and death,
the trials of the body and the brain.
To say, when our health goes south,
'No, not this.'

> *As he follows his route through the hospital*
> *it begins to come to life around him.*
> *Nurses doing handovers, radiographers preparing,*
> *domestics delivering meals, doctors reading notes.*

Ever since then, I'd say, all of us
who work in medicine,
well, we're all, however tangential,
descendants aren't we?
Of that offering, that first intimate action.

Here in Wales, by all accounts, we started early.
Around 1000 BC, before Hippocrates, mind,
that's when *Meddyginiaeth* – medicine,
or the language of doctors, literally –
was first recorded as a rural art,

practised by the *Cymro* before they had much
of anything else – cities, sovereignty.
By 430 BC it lay even closer
to the civic heart, protected and encouraged
as one of three civil arts.

> *YVONNE, a domestic,*
> *is buffing the corridor between two wards.*

Yvonne

It was, fair dos – but what were the other two?
Navigation, that was one and Commerce the other.
Oh yeah, right from the start
money and medicine were close, like brothers.

Just look at the laws of Hywel Dda,
in what, 930 AD? There it is in black and white,

'the offices of the court physician'.
But what else did those laws enshrine? That's right. His fees.

'Four pence for the letting of blood
Nine score and his food for a dangerous wound –
a stroke on the head unto the brain,
a stroke on the body unto the bowels,
a broken limb put right –
Four pence again for herbs to ease a pain.
Twelve pence for an ointment of red.
One legal penny for his light every night
and one and a half for his daily bread.'

HYWEL has collected
an elderly patient, ALICE.
As he wheels her back to her ward—

Hywel

She's right of course. There's no denying,
the ideas that make us meet in us too,
conjoin, get all wrapped up in each other,
until to imagine them apart, pulled asunder,
well, would be more vision than thought.

I mean, time, knowledge, skill,
none has ever come for nothing has it?
So how might you do it? Where would you begin?
To unwrap the money from the medicine?
Make individual care a communal concern?

How might you surgically remove
financial transaction from the consulting room?
Make treatments free at the point of care,
available to all, no matter who they are?
Would it even be possible?

HYWEL rolls ALICE into her ward,
handing over to VALERIA, a nurse.
As he leaves—

Good questions, all,
but before you can solve them
you need someone to ask them
and that, I'd argue, is when sometimes
one person can be the difference.

Not to *have* the idea as such, but yes,
to change its direction, maybe, who knows,
even where it lands, the final destination.
Someone who doesn't just see the vision
but who can raise it too,

beyond the orbit of the eye
towards the doing of the hand
and the believing of the brain.

YVONNE is storing her buffer in a storage cupboard.
As she emerges—

Yvonne

It can happen.
Look at Churchill during the war.
Everyone knew what had to be done,
but to get us there?

That took a certain sort of man,
someone who could imagine the journey
and in that imagining make it happen.
Which he did. But after war comes peace,

a very different proposition.
And harder too, perhaps,
to win your victories not on the field of battle
but in the day-to-day lives of your people.

HYWEL joins her.

Hywel

But that can be done too, can't it?
And that's the tale, if you'll listen, we'll tell.
The story of how, in the wake of a war,
we came as a country to care how we do.
How, seventy years ago, all this began
– not the idea born fully formed in the mind of one man
but yes, it becoming tangible through his action.

Yvonne

Nye. Aneurin Bevan. Born not far from here,
just over those hills, up in Tredegar.
Which is where the story starts, really.

Because it was that town what made him, wasn't it?
With its mix of workers, libraries, family.
The forging and breaking of men in the mine's abyss.

Hywel

And his parents too, mind. Their influence.
But yeah, all that, his early fuel, it made it possible, didn't it?
For him in turn to give us this.

The Voice of Aneurin Bevan (13 December 1945)

'As I see it, the undertaking to provide all
    people
with all kinds of health care
calls for something bolder than mere adaptation.
For here is an opportunity which may not recur
for a thorough reconstruction
of the country's health position.'

Birth

from that once-imagining

There is no more pleasant sight to be seen in
the world than can be seen outside a maternity
clinic in Great Britain today, where women of
all classes in the community mingle together,
taking their children to be weighed and to be
examined, to receive their lessons in maternal
care, to have advice about what food to give
their children, and to listen to the doctors'
advice as to what may be wrong with them.

— Aneurin Bevan,
House of Commons, July 1958

Early morning.
ANEIRA, seventy years old, is sitting at a table
in her home in Loughor, near Swansea.

Aneira

I was the seventh child,
born last, so never knew
my grandmothers, see?

One died at thirty-three, the other forty-four,
years before Mam had me.
Was a neighbour who delivered

my brothers and sisters.
But then that's how it used to be,
wasn't it? For most, before.

A woman in the community
with some years and common sense,
that's who brought us into the world.

Or didn't, as was sometimes the case.

MATTHEW, a retired neurosurgeon,
is getting dressed in his bedroom.

Matthew

My father was a doctor, and his father
before him a surgeon. So, to tell the truth
I'm not sure I ever had a choice.

It always seemed to be my destination
and in my family, school, well,
let's just say no one got rewarded for hesitation.

I can tell you, though, when all that changed,
when it went from being a familial duty
to something more, well, fundamental.

The first time I saw a human brain.
I was training, only observing,
but the consultant, he told me to come closer,

lean in, take a look. And there it was,
the most beautiful thing I'd ever seen.
This glistening, pulsating mass, this thought made flesh.

It's who we are, isn't it? And yet at the same time,
so unknown, as mysterious, really, as the deepest ocean.
And yet vital – as in *vitae*. Life. The soul even, perhaps.

From then on, for me, there was no question.

SIAN, a nurse, takes over from the night shift
in the Special Care Baby Unit.

Sian

No one medical in my family.
No nurses, doctors, but when my daughter was little,
she was ill, see?

Only meant to be in for three or four days
but in the end it was more like eleven.
Anyway, there was one nurse, Rose was her name,

and oh, she was marvellous.
The care she gave my little girl! And to me.
It was frightening, make no mistake,

but she always explained what was happening, see?
Always took her time, gave us comfort,
but was straight with us too.

I never forgot her and twelve years later,
well, I done my own training.
So yeah, it's because of Rose, that's why I'm here.

> *ELUNED is preparing her artist materials at a life class.*
> *The model in the centre of the room*
> *is a heavily pregnant woman.*

Eluned

I was pregnant with our second

13

when at twenty-eight weeks one night
I started to bleed. There was pain too.

I didn't know what to do.
My husband was working away, so,
well, I'd never done it before,

but for the very first time I dialled 999.
And they came. They were so calm,
the ambulance men. Talked me down,

told me everything would be alright,
put me in the back, then, with one of them
holding my hand, drove off at speed, into the night.

                    GWYN is walking in the hills.

Gwyn

We've all been in contact with it,
of course we have. I mean,
we're born into it, aren't we?

From our very first breaths.
But that said, for most of us,
through our younger adult years,

I'd say it probably seems a bit distant.
A story in the press, usually bad,
the odd appointment with a doctor.

But then you have kids and all that changes,
even without things going wrong. You become aware,
don't you? Of this vast connective tissue of care.

This population of nurses, physios, doctors, surgeons
all there for the health of your child;
a department or specialist for every inch of their body,

their lungs, heart, eyes, kidneys.
It's humbling, but I won't lie,
that night I found it frightening too.

I mean, they were in danger,
that's how it felt. Both of them – their lives
in the hands of a system, strangers.

> *ELUNED sits in A&E.*
> *A midwife, WENDY, sits with her, holding her hand.*

Eluned

There were no beds in maternity,
so they put me in a cubicle in A&E.
It wasn't ideal, I know,

but the midwife I'd first seen,
she stayed with me. She didn't have to
and I could see she was busy, but she did.

Sat with me there, just holding my hand
while I cried, not knowing if the daughter
inside me was alive or had died.

Gwyn

By the time I got there it was morning.
I'd driven through the night
and came in running.

At that point I was, well,
scared I guess. For my wife
and the life that she held.

Our first, you see,
he was born at home,
under midwife care, but there,

among our sofas and chairs.
We'd hoped for the same again,
so this – this wasn't part of the plan.

Eluned

I remember, when Gwyn arrived for the scan,
holding his hand so tightly our knuckles went white
as we waited for that screen to translate sound into light
and show us what would come next.

It held so much, that one machine, and we could feel it.
The fate of our daughter who, if she survived,
would one day love, imagine, dream and be.
Or wouldn't. Because of course that's what else

was held in that screen – as they lifted my gown
and squeezed out the gel – the possibility
that all that future life – hers and ours – had already,
at home, in the ambulance, in A&E, bled out of me.

WENDY, *the midwife,*
sits in the 'cwtch' *room in maternity.*

Wendy

The NHS, it's there for when the pattern breaks, isn't it?
When the day we expect, the story we're living
whoever you are,
takes a turn we didn't see coming.

Being a midwife, people often say,
'You're lucky, you're at the other end of all that.
You bring the turn everyone wants –
new life in the room, two people arriving, three going out.'

And it's true, mostly we do. And that's amazing.
It gets me every time, that creation of joy.
That simple thought, each time one's born,
what life will they have, this girl, this boy?

But birth, well, sometimes I think that's a story
we expect to run too easy, and it isn't always like that.
You'd be surprised, how often it doesn't work out.
When that happens though, there's still care to be given,

I'd say more perhaps. What do I do? What else?

17

I cry with them. Give them a *cwtch*.
I mean, we're not robots are we? And at that moment,
for them, the worst has happened.

We can't make that better but we *can*
change the quality of what they'll remember.
And that's caring too – not just for now, but also their future.
How? Well, for a start I'll ask if we can call it by name,

the baby, and if there's no foetal heart, encourage a natural
    delivery.
That sounds cruel, I know, but it means leaving no scar
and the mothers, they should have a choice, shouldn't they?
In the future, if they want to remember or not?

It's why we made a special exit, so they don't have to pass
the newborns in the cots. And why we make a memory box too,
whether the baby's over twenty-four weeks and registered, or
    under and not.
Just a few things – a lock of hair, prints of their hands and feet,

a star to hang on the tree, a teddy bear. And photos, we take
    those too.
The mothers don't always want them, but later,
nearly all come back for them. Maybe a year or so after,
or sometimes more – five, ten. They come in,

and Kerry'll look through the notes and find them –
their baby, there, in the world, making its mark, however
    briefly.

To be fair, she's been instrumental in all this, Kerry.
She does the most—

Kerry

              —not the most, that's not right.
But yeah, I did feel there was a role for me there.
I'm the secretary, see? Admin support.
But if I could turn back the clock, well,
I think my real passion would have been nursing, care.
I've come to love it, however hard it might be;

the patient contact, and being able to help when, well,
it must be so difficult, mustn't it? To have made this life
and then suddenly . . . I guide them through the process,
the funeral, cremation – all paid for by the health board,
   mind –
prepare the father for what he might be asked,
if he wants to carry the coffin, that kind of thing.

We offer the option of a cold cot too,
for when the mother isn't ready for the goodbyes just yet.
To keep the body from, well, you know . . .
It's a big help that, being able to say, 'Yes,
stay with your baby if you want,'
and not just for minutes, but for days instead.

Eluned

I knew before they turned the screen to us.
The midwife, it was written on her face.
And sure enough, when they did, she was there –

Our daughter, the white of her in all that fluid black,
her palm blooming briefly against the amniotic sac,
as if to say, 'Don't worry, Mum, I'm still here.'

Gwyn

But so was something else.
More black, pools of it throughout the placenta,
like lakes on a map.

A bleed, that's what they called it after.
A haemorrhage, making the womb
more ticking bomb than cosy home.

It all happened quickly after that.
Thirty, forty minutes later
and they had us all in theatre.

HYWEL pushes ELUNED on a bed.
WENDY and GWYN walk beside.

Hywel

'*What is now proved was once, only imagined.*'
A good line that – William Blake's though, not mine.
Fitting enough I suppose, for all this.

Except of course it gives no sense, does it?
Of how difficult it was – to birth such a happening
from that once-imagining.

To make the attempt
after centuries of wealth meaning health,
to do things differently, begin again.

So, where to start then? In telling *that* story?
With the child maybe, the 'father of the man'
who would, in turn, play midwife to that birth.

                         Nye. Aneurin Bevan.

Born the sixth of ten he was, in a two-up two-down—

                   YVONNE, pushing a cleaning trolley.

Yvonne

                 —No, got to go deeper than that!
Deeper than family. I mean,
think of the *soul* of that town at that time –
the spirit of his generation.

A culture of communal ambition
in which power was a vehicle for ideas
and ideas close cousins of action.

A desire to rise not out of your class, but *with* it.
To make collective contribution
a source of individual emancipation.

A belief in a civilised society
in terms of wealth, health and beauty,
for all and not just the few.

A youth of such texture that the questions posed
by him and his peers weren't so much personal,
as communal of value – Not what shall *I be*,

or what career should I choose,
but what, to make the world better,
shall *we do*?

Hywel

But look what he had inside the home, too.
His father, a miner but also a poet, a reader,
and like so many others in the valleys back then
a Liberal voter turned recently Labour.

While in his mother a frugal, capable force of nature,
possessed of a will she passed on to her son
who from early on, though fettered by a stutter,
would never run short on thoughts, speech, opinion.

Yvonne

And beyond that home, Tredegar –
a town in a company's grip,
and at the contested heart of both – the pit.

The young Nye went down it early,
at just thirteen, working the seam
of a mine called *Ty Trist* –

'House of Sadness' that meant – and it was,
no denying, a hard way to live.

But for him it was a house of learning, too.
Because it was *there*, see, in the mines,
that his natural leanings – to pursue change,
expect more for all, to challenge authority –

found a clear and present enemy
on which to focus –
the Tredegar Iron and Coal Company.

Hywel

At nineteen he became the youngest lodge leader ever,
taking them to task over rights, efficiency, pay,
then not long after, as a councillor,

he was after them again – over housing,
health, sanitation, water.
He founded a club with like-minded friends,

the Query they called it, and fuelled
by the socialist ideas of the day,
they made it their aim to make things better,

first in Tredegar, then Wales, then the world.
Their lives, you see, were living descriptions
of the philosophies they'd read on paper –

industry, poverty, a debilitating inequality
and a workforce ruled by the owners
not just in the mines but in their homes as well.

So, secretly at first, these Query boys
began to make their ways
into the local engines of change –

the boards, the party, the councils, the committees –
disturbing as they did, the established scene –
the Guardians, the Federation, and yes, the company.

'There isn't room,' its manager once said to Nye,
'in this company for you and me.' 'I know,'
he replied, 'which is why you should go.'

Yvonne

At the age of twenty-six he added to his list
the Tredegar Medical Aid Society,
serving on its hospitals committee.

Every miner in the area,
in return for two- or threepence a week,
got health care, free at the point of delivery –

a choice of five or six doctors,
the services of specialists, hospital facilities.
It was far from perfect, but as a glimpse

of how things could be?
How communal action might set the individual free?
There it was, in front of Bevan, in practice, not theory.

Financial concern at times of injury, sickness,

removed from working-class homes.
The health of each person, through shared contribution,
no longer a weight to be carried alone.

Hywel

When not engaged in his public works, he escaped,
when he could, into books from the library –
which, incidentally, as chairman
he built into one of the best in the country –

or up into the hills of the Breconshire border
to tramp the plateaus above Tredegar
talking politics with his friend Archie Lush,
or, to soothe his stutter, reciting poetry, Shakespeare.

Yvonne

Ideas, conviction, vision –
they all need a soil in which to be sown
and for Bevan, this was his.

Hywel

And what fertile soil it was, this hinterland
of the young MP, who after years of opposition
found himself, in the wake of a terrible war,

tasked by Clement Attlee, his new prime minister,
with both housing a bombed-out Britain
and creating, from the drained public purse,

a health service fit for the nation.

Yvonne

And if it hadn't been?
If the formative soil of the minister for health
at that time and place

had been of a different constitution,
then what? Well, if you ask me,
one thing's for certain,

the shape and nature of all this,
which we now consider a part of us,
would have been very different.

And so would we.

Aneira

There's a story my mother used to tell
about when her father was carried home,
his leg broken down the mine.

How when the doctor came,
'Come on children,' he said,
'help me hold your father down.'

So they did, there on the kitchen table,
which is where, without anaesthetic,
he operated.

I think we forget, sometimes,
what it could be like.

Not that my mother could.

'Darling,' she'd say to me,
more and more towards the end,
'I can still hear those screams.'

She was a pianist, Mam.
I've got her diploma upstairs.
So imagine how it must have been

when two days later,
with all the kids crying,
the same men as carried in their father,

carried out their piano.
They were poor, see,
had to pay the doctor.

Kerry

I just feel lucky I can do it all on the NHS.
I mean, imagine, if at times like this
I was asking the parents about money, insurance.
We're meant to be easing the pain, not causing distress.

It's about gifting people time, isn't it?
And not just Mum and Dad, either. I mean,
I've known nurses, midwives in here,
who when a baby won't survive,

and the mother would rather not see, or can't,

will take that foetus while still alive
and just *cwtch* it close in a corner –
until its heart stops beating or the breaths stop coming,

so for those few seconds it can feel human warmth
and what it's like, I suppose, to be who we are.
But things like that, they happen all the time –
in ambulances, people's homes, GPs' surgeries –

thousands of moments of quiet care,
every minute of every day. And not extraordinary, either.
Because at its best that's what it is, isn't it? The NHS.
Compassion being just the way things are.

> *ANVI, a consultant obstetrician, is scrubbing up,*
> *preparing to perform ELUNED's C-section.*

Anvi

I remember, as a child, in India,
my mother would ask us to pray
for the women in labour.

If they needed a caesarean,
you see, there was no facility.
Sometimes just to bleed could be fatal.

The hospital was hers, she set it up –
a nursing home for pregnant women
in a place called Kinnigoli.

The first time she visited me, she was shocked.
'Is this really,' she said, 'the NHS?
God! Look at the curtains!'

We'd heard so much, see,
about the NHS, in India,
and there, well, private practice, it's very posh.

So I had to explain to her.
'Yes, Mummy,' I said. 'It is.
And yes, I know the building is old,

but all this care – the latest machines, the drugs,
the bloods – it's free, and that, not the curtains,
is where you look for the beauty.'

Hywel

The election that brought Labour to power
was an election like no other.
The public made their voices clear –
they said goodbye to Churchill,

their greatest war leader ever,
and voted instead for change, a new way of being.
After six years of fighting they wanted to see
the national energy they'd witnessed

turned to the work of peace – a welfare state,
a new society. Labour had the majority, the country.
Added to this was a cross-party consensus

for the creation of a national health service.

Provision had been growing, but slowly.
It was patchwork at best and still left most people paying.
A confusion of local authorities, private doctors,
approved societies. There was no cohesion and now,

after what had been proved in the war –
how when we had to we could come together –
that's what everyone wanted.
So yes, Bevan assumed his position

against a background of agreement.
His Tory predecessor, Willink, had published
a white paper – *A National Health Service*.
So again, yes, whoever had won the election

would have made an attempt.
But still, the landscape before Bevan,
that was, well, more difficult . . .
What hadn't been agreed on, see, was the *extent*
to which the idea would be driven,

and on that front, he had his work cut out.

HYWEL passes ELUNED on to the theatre staff.

Yvonne

From the off, there were two clear obstacles.
The first of these was the hospitals.

All previous plans for a national service
had them staying under current control,
be that voluntary or local authority.

But Nye, well, he wanted more than that,
a service owned by the public – national
not just in geography, but also universality.
Excellence for everybody.
That meant consultants spread throughout the country,

attracted to local jobs by secure, long-term salaries.
And it meant organisational unity, too,
the many working as one in as fluid a way as possible.
Only the state could achieve all that, pay those bills,
so for Nye there was only one solution – nationalise the
   hospitals.

There was outcry. From local authorities, doctors,
politicians and press. No one had ever imagined
a minister doing *this*. Churchill was critical
and Willink, too – 'The plan would,' he said,
'destroy so much in this country that we value.'

Nye had to fight for it – and not just against the Tories,
but also in cabinet. But he won. Which for him was vital,
and not just because it was practical,
but also because for Bevan, as ever,
there was something else at stake – a moral principle.

The Voice of Aneurin Bevan

'It is repugnant to a civilised community
for hospitals to rely on private charity.
I have always felt a shudder of repulsion
when I have seen nurses, sisters,
who ought to be at their work . . .
going about the streets collecting for
hospitals.'

HYWEL is on a break in the porters' coffee room.

Hywel

Having secured his plan Bevan fine-tuned the Bill,
adding dental, ophthalmic and hearing to the scheme,
all to be offered on the very first day. As ever,
it was important to him that change happened *now*.

Mental health, too, for the very first time,
would be part of the service with immediate effect.
As he said, 'The separation of mental from physical treatment
is a source of endless cruelty and neglect.'

Not that there weren't concessions – there were,
such as specialists treating hospital patients
who'd still pay fees. Nothing else, he said,
caused him more anxiety.

But if Bevan was a dreamer, he was practical too,
always pursuing the principle of action, so he knew

it was vital – keeping those specialists, the consultants,
inside the system would ensure its survival.

ELUNED is in her life class.

Eluned

There were complications with the spinal
so, quite quickly, they had to put me under.
I remember the anaesthetist talking to me,
his voice fading away, and all the time,
as the world became blurred,
this burning concern for my baby.
Will she survive? If she does, will she be okay?

The last thing I remember, though,
was something I held, not heard. A hand,
I still don't know whose, but someone, a nurse,
one of the team, had come to sit beside me.
A man, I think, from the texture of his palm.
I squeezed it tight and in some way that helped –
a human anchor, a compassionate tether,
as I slipped away, into a chemical night.

GWYN is walking in the hills.

Gwyn

I've never felt, at once, such gratitude and dread –
thankful my wife and daughter were there
receiving the care, the procedure they needed,

but fearful, too, at what the outcome might be.
Then suddenly, there was a midwife at the door.
'Come on,' she said, 'time to meet your daughter, Dad.'

When I first saw her, she was in a side room,
her chest rapid with her lungs,
lying on her back between two paediatricians.

There were nurses in there too,
and in the theatre beyond six, seven more staff.
She seemed so small, of no size at all

to be at the centre of so many,
but there she was, alive. 'Can I pick her up?'
I asked. 'Yes, of course,' the doctors said,

one from Vietnam, I think, the other, Syria.
For a moment we all just looked at her.
Life, brought into the room.

But then she started changing colour.
'She's going dusky,' someone said, and seconds later
she was being rushed up the corridor,

nurses running with her incubator.
For the briefest of moments she'd been in my arms
but then, just minutes old, and once again the system had her.

YVONNE is pushing her cleaning trolley
through the wards.

Yvonne

That second obstacle on the horizon before Bevan
was the doctors themselves –
the British Medical Association.

For eighteen months they locked horns with him,
sceptical of the service he was planning.
The negotiations were gruelling,

across thirty-one meetings the BMA
pressed home their points of opposition,
stoked by the right-wing press,

who painted Nye as loud-mouthed, uncouth.
For many their fears were genuine,
their complaints, they felt, a defence

of their Hippocratic oath. Where Bevan
saw reform, you see, they saw a darker fate –
a loss of medical freedom in a totalitarian state,

doctors as civil servants, unable to name their price
and GPs no longer allowed
to buy and sell their practice.

In public then, 'Bevan versus the BMA'
became a favourite headline of the day,
creating cold feet in government

and fuelling the firepower of Churchill,

who saw the cabinet's youngest member – 'a squalid nuisance'
as he called him – as Labour's Achilles heel as well.

In private, however, around the negotiating table
and then again over drinks or dinner,
Nye steered a more nuanced, considered course.

Aggressive one day, conciliatory the next,
deploying both the carrot of concessions
and the stick of the constitutional point

that as an interest group the BMA
could never actually stop the Act
and nor, Bevan knew, would they want to.

I mean, imagine that – the doctors
being the sole reason why the public,
sisters, nurses couldn't have their service.

> *HYWEL pushes a young boy with a broken leg to X-ray.*

Hywel

When, in January '48, just six months before
the Act's implementation date,
the BMA passed a motion of no confidence,

Bevan knew he had to find a way through.
His tactic was to appeal to the individual,
the doctors themselves not their association,

who had, he said, in terms of the Act,
only been interested in misrepresentation.
But the doctor alone, the GP, the surgeon,

they would, he was sure, when presented with the facts
see the benefits for them and their patients.
So, gambling on keeping to the day

when the Act would come into effect,
Bevan gave a speech, in February of '48,
in which he let fly at the BMA,

proving, one by one, their fears
to be phantom, before concluding
with a 'sad reflection':

The Voice of Aneurin Bevan

'That this great Act . . . should have so stormy
  a birth.
We all hoped it would have excited
the medical profession -
that despite our economic anxieties
we are still able to do
the most civilised thing in the world,
and put the welfare of the sick
before every other consideration.'

Yvonne

Together with more minor concessions
Bevan's tactics worked, and by that May
the BMA had advised the profession
to work with the service coming into being.

Somehow he'd done it – against a weight
of sceptical opposition, including the Tories
voting twenty-two times against the Act –
in a couple of years he'd brought about

a drastic shift in the country's cultural position.
Health care free at the point of delivery
would, in a matter of months, become a right,
an expectation.

So much more, then, than just a political victory.
No, all this, it was about more than that,
as Bevan himself said on the eve of the Act.
'We now,' he told the crowd,

speaking at a rally in Manchester,
'have the moral leadership of the world.'
Moral, again. This was always, you see,
for Bevan about one thing –

poverty and the shadow it brings,
and our ability as a species to work together,
if we want to, to make that shadow
just a little bit lighter.

The Voice of Aneurin Bevan

'I believe it will lift the shadow from millions
  of homes.
It will keep very many people alive who might
  otherwise be dead.
It will relieve suffering.
It will produce higher standards for the medical
  profession.
It will be a great contribution towards the
wellbeing of the common people of Great Britain.'

> *SIAN is in the Special Care Baby Unit*
> *tending to premature newborns.*

Sian

It is hard for the parents, course it is.
I mean, they're stressed as hell, their baby's come early
or with complications, so more vulnerable, probably,
than at any other time in its life. So yes, of course
they want to be close to them, giving the care.
But lots of the time they can't, that has to be us.

I'll be honest, just after I started I almost gave up.
It was too stressful – the long shifts, then, when we lost
  one . . .
You can't just leave that sort of thing at the door.
But my family, they told me to stick at it,
and I'm glad they did. Because I love my job, I do.
Still stressful, of course. I mean, look at this,

so much new life in one room, and some of it
hanging by just a thread, too – and not just the baby's
but the parents', the families'. All in our hands.
It's worth it though. I mean, sometimes I think, in here,
this place, it's the best embodiment of the NHS.
These babies, they're from every background –

well-to-do, valleys, poor, well off.
All got different lives ahead of them too, and yeah,
the playing fields will get unlevel, all too soon.
By the age of three, for many, their life will be set,
and mostly by money. But in here, see? They all get the same
    care,
regardless who they are. And that, that really matters to me.

Gwyn

When I next saw her
she was in one of the cots
in the Special Care Unit,

her body covered in tubes –
one up her nose, another in her hand,
a mask on her face.

There at her head, though,
already on a label
with a cartoon of Alice in Wonderland,

was her name – Siriol.
Which is when it came clear.

Yes, the system had her

but it was holding her too,
as an individual. A person,
newly through the looking glass

into this world of us.
And not only that,
but here she was at that moment,

along with my wife being stitched
two floors below,
the most precious things in my life,

and yet not once, despite that value,
had anyone mentioned money, payment.
And for that, too, I felt grateful.

Not because I wouldn't have paid it –
of course I would.
But that's the point. Others couldn't.

And even if they could,
it would be so easy to exploit,
wouldn't it? Health. Love.

But there, in the NHS,
no one does. And that, I'd say,
more than anything else, speaks well of us.

Aneira

Well, you can imagine,
after six kids my mother was used
to hearing someone say, 'Push! Push!'
But not with me.

This was July 4th 1948, see?
Well, the doctor, he was determined
to deliver the first NHS baby,
and in Wales too, in Swansea.

So 'Hold on, Edna, hold on,'
that's what he said, as the hands of the clock
moved closer together.
Until around midnight, when at last

my mam was allowed to push instead.
Two minutes past, on the 5th,
that's when I was born.
He named me too, that doctor.

'There's only one name for her,'
that's what he said. 'Aneira.'

MATTHEW is in his kitchen at home.

Matthew

Yes, I do remember in fact,
when the Act came into effect.
Or at least, I remember when I first
realised what that meant.

I must have been eight, nine,
early autumn, starting school,
when I walked into the dining room
to find the table empty, which was unusual.

Every quarter, you see,
my father would use that table
to lay out his bills before sending them out.
It became a 'thing', I suppose,

something my mother complained about.
Except then, in the autumn of '48,
she didn't have to any more,
because they were gone, weren't they?

Now, it would be a mistake, of course,
to pretend it was all as simple as that.
That before July 5th everyone paid,
and after they didn't.

My father was always saying
how patients still got treated for free before –
via charities, the panel, or through
doctors playing Robin Hood,

offering their services gratis
to those who couldn't pay,
then charging those who could.
But at the same time, well,

it can't be denied, can it?
That relationship between patient
and doctor, the country
and health care, whether old or young,

rich or poor, infirm or able,
it altered overnight.
The best of medicine for everyone,
no longer a luxury but a right.

And taken off the table
those bills, that money,
and with them so much else –
inequality, stress, avoidance, worry.

Life

these chains of care

This Service must always be changing, growing
and improving; it must always appear to be
inadequate.

— Aneurin Bevan,
25 June 1948

A district nurse enters a home.
A mental health practitioner gets into their car.
An ambulance pulls out of a bay.
Patients arrive in a GP's waiting room.
The lights of an operating theatre switch on.
A pharmacy robot tracks long walls of medication.
X-rays are illuminated, blood cells appear under a microscope.
A cardiogram pulses.

Thank-you cards are pinned to noticeboards
in several departments.
A whiteboard is filled with the names of patients.

JANICE, a middle-aged woman, is sitting in a cubicle in A&E.

Janice

I worked in America for a bit
and was ill a few times while there.

The first question they always asked
was about insurance, how I'd pay.

When I came in here that day,
I thought about that again.

How different it was, when the triage nurse,
before anything else, asked me first,

Valeria

So, what's your name?

> *EVA, nine years old, plays in the waiting room*
> *of the children's centre.*
> *Her mother, BETHAN, reads a magazine.*

Eva

I was born with a genetic disorder.
It's got several names.
Deletion syndrome is one.
DiGeorge another.

They all mean the same thing, though.
Thirty or forty deleted genes
from one of my chromosomes.
Number 22, to be exact.

And, well, lots of possible symptoms.
Mine are mostly with immunity,
and language too, which is one of the clinics
I've got today – speech therapy.

Bethan

They diagnosed her in the womb,
then induced her straight away.
We didn't have any time to think.
It was all such a shock.
The midwives were amazing though,
and the doctors, from the off.

And by doctors, I mean a lot.
With this syndrome, you see,
the issues are multifarious,
can affect nearly every organ,
every system. Heart, kidneys,
cleft palate, ENT.

What was incredible was that
from the moment it was diagnosed
we had access to all of these
specialists in every field –
cardiology, endocrine.
It was pretty overwhelming.

> *VIJAY, a junior doctor,*
> *is cycling into the hospital through town.*

Vijay

I was applying for uni in 2007, 8
and heading for the City. But then the market crashed,
people were losing their jobs and, well,
the world of finance didn't look so pretty.

So I did some work experience
shadowing across a range of specialties –
theatre, outpatients, on the wards. I enjoyed it all
but what drew me was the culture, the team camaraderie

and everyone bonded by this common goal.
I found it infectious, the mentality, a shared desire to care.

I took a step out in my second year,
did a management course and it was that,

the culture I missed. So that's why I'm still here.
Don't get me wrong, lots of reasons not to be.
The hours, the pressure, but look at this,
these places, they're the most equal,

democratic and diverse we've got,
and no one after your money when you walk
through the door. Where else does that happen?
Maybe universities, once, but not any more.

So yeah, I'd say it's the best of us, the NHS.
It's not perfect, I know, but it's still world-class –
a beautiful idea made manifest.
Where else can you say you're part of something like that?

> *RAV, a young consultant neurosurgeon,*
> *is arriving for his shift at a specialist unit in Cardiff.*

Rav

As is so often the case
I inherited my interest from someone else,
a consultant who trained me.

You hear of that again and again –
you're a young doctor, trying things out,
then you meet a certain surgeon, a specialist,

who somehow makes their subject
light up, make sense. For me, it was the brain.
The way Matthew spoke about it

with such reverence.
So I hope I'm doing the same, now,
with my own students.

Passing on, down the chain
not just knowledge, but passion.

KEMI, a junior doctor,
is revising for an exam at home.

Kemi

I was always interested in the science of it
but decided to train more for that other aspect –
the people.

I don't know, it's about wanting to serve, I suppose;
put my shoulder to the wheel
and in doing so

be part of the world that heals, not hurts.

Bethan

In the first year of her life,
Eva had fifty appointments.
As they ticked things off the list,
these got less. But yes,

she'll always have those –
dates for scans, check-ups, tests.

It's defined where we'll live.
My husband's Irish and we
were thinking of moving there,
but without the NHS, well,
I just don't see how that's possible.
Imagine the cost, because to get insurance . . .

And it's not just that.
The best treatment, you see,
for this syndrome, is multidisciplinary.
And that's something else
you get with the NHS – collaboration,
the internal communication.

A pair of A&E consultants, RACHEL and GIOVANNI,
are manipulating JANICE's wrist.

Janice

There had been thunderstorms,
so it was slippery, the paving stone.
I fell and broke my wrist, the radial bone.

This was on a bank holiday
so the waiting room was heaving,
but still, the staff kept up this, well, quiet efficiency.

When the doctor saw me she explained

that rather go for a plate or pins,
she and a colleague would manipulate the bone back in.

To watch them – it was fascinating. Like choreography,
    almost.
They had a trust, you could see, born, I guess,
from seeing the worst together, but also the best.

Giovanni

Having an immediate effect, that's what I like.
People present with a pain – in their chest, their leg,
their head – and in the best cases
you take it away, and when you do
you see them come back to you.

VIJAY is checking on ALICE.

Vijay

And more I'd say, their past and future too.
Pain, you see, especially acute or chronic,
it folds you in, until all you have is the present.

You ease it, and for the patient time grows again
and with it the imagination –
who they can be, what might they do.

Which is why it's so hard when you can't.
Ease it I mean. As a junior doctor, you care
for lots of end-of-life patients and there are some,
I can see them now, they couldn't even talk to me

53

or move even, because of the morphine,
but it was in their eyes, the suffering.

My job was to keep them alive, comfortable, breathing.
But yeah, sometimes you do find yourself asking,
is that, in this case, the most humane thing?

> *KAREN, a GP, is in her consulting room.*

Karen

Pain, in some ways, it makes us more animal again.
That immediacy, the inward vision.
In the release, well, we become more human, outward-
    looking.

Working here for so many years,
seeing so many stories of suffering, healing
walk through these doors, I'd say that's one of the ways

the NHS performs. By releasing or easing all that pain
it enables a society, a nation, to become as a whole
more human. Those stories, though – it's those that stay with me.

The idea that here, as a GP, I'm at the beginning
of so many; a gatekeeper, really,
with the whole system before me.

Giovanni

Children are the best to bring back from pain –
they smile, play again, become who they are.

I love that. Which is why I could never,
I think, work in paediatrics. That emotional stress,
of treating a child who may never be well, or worse . . .

> *A six-year-old boy*
> *is rushed into A&E, unconscious.*

Although, of course, we see that here too,
but somehow, it's different. A&E, in this way, it's unique.
In other departments, people arrive with a diagnosis.
Here, though, especially when the case is acute,
we have to do both at once – diagnose and treat.
Work out what's wrong, and for the next ten minutes,
just get them through. So yes, no denying,
it's that urgency I love about this job – stopping people dying.

Rachel

And the variety of people you meet.
I mean, let's face it, the NHS has two front doors –
the GPs and us. This is where you enter it,
straight off the street. Demand is up, no doubt,
especially during winter pressures,

but the real problem is cuts, capacity – I mean,
ten years ago we had a third more beds
and over that same decade drastic cuts to social care,
year on year. So where do you think picks up on that slack?
Yeah, too right, places like here.

The NHS – it was designed as part of a system,

a network of welfare. But I don't know,
it feels more and more now like an island,
an island of care marooned in a wider society
that doesn't any more. Don't get me wrong –

I love my job, all of us do. You kind of have to!
In some ways it's primitive medicine, raw,
and yeah, you can feel exposed, especially at nights,
on your own with patients flooding the door.
But at the same time you've got the whole hospital

at your back, on call, and when the team come together,
on a resus or similar, well, there's nothing like it –
the ultimate hive brain, everything done in
parallel, each with their job, but working as one.
I don't know, we're always being told

the NHS can learn from industry,
but I'd say it's the other way round.
The altruism of the staff, their loyalty –
if an industry could foster that . . .
that would be one hell of a company.

> *The six-year-old boy goes into cardiac arrest.*
> *The crash team goes to work, led by GIOVANNI.*

> *STEVE, a cardiothoracic surgeon, is operating on a heart.*

Steve

When a heart arrests, it often doesn't stop.

But what does happen is a fatal change in its rhythm.
The electrical charge that makes the muscle move

goes from a smooth, regular pattern to no pattern at all –
chaotic. This means the heart is no longer efficient,
and therefore no longer feeding blood to the brain.

And that can be it – the difference between
someone being here and not. Electricity and rhythm,
our rhythm – that's what starts us, and can make us stop.

> *BILL, an anaesthetist, sits at the head of a patient*
> *under general.*

Bill

It's all physics, really, anaesthetics.
The science of flow, the heart a pump, the pressures.
Like flying a plane, that's how some describe it.

Most of your time you're watching the dials,
monitors – take-off and landing,
that's the tricky bit.

For me though, it's about another kind of flow as well –
relationships. Between you and the patient, firstly.
I mean, they're anxious, of course they are –

this, your day job is, for them, a significant moment,
perhaps once in a lifetime. So you talk to them, keep them
    calm.

Then there's the flow between you and your surgeon.

If you know each other, then things just go better.
I can adjust my doses to the way they work
so a patient will wake up crisper, and if things go wrong,

which yes, they sometimes do, then, well,
if you have those years of working together
they go a lot less wrong than they could do.

> MELISSA, *a vascular nurse, is on a community visit,*
> *walking down a street to a patient's home.*

Melissa

I specialise in end-stage renal, diabetes, dialysis,
and have done for years now. I run an emergency clinic,
mostly for limb salvage, but do this a lot too,
community visits. Some of my patients,
they can no longer leave home, so yeah, I come to them.
They're mostly old, often alone. It is shocking,
sometimes, to see how they're living.

A stint in hospital, though,
and they come out looking brilliant –
washed, hair cut, fed three times a day.
Then a month later and they'll be back to square one again.
It is frustrating, not having the access to put them right,
but if they don't want to engage, change . . .
When I was younger it was a real education.

I mean, you grow up thinking people are like you,
have the same opportunities but then,
those first years of district nursing, the things I saw.
Frightening, too, sometimes. Intimidating.
It still isn't easy. You get close to patients, don't you?
And in this area, vascular, well, expectation is low.
After losing one leg, they'll usually, in a year or two,

lose the second, and after that, well . . .
What's surprising is how few even realise,
when they first come in, that they could lose a limb,
through diabetes, I mean. It might be a wound,
or some discolouration,
but if we can't get the bloods in, and fast,
then there's nothing else for it but amputation.

> *BILL is preparing for his next operation.*

Bill

Working somewhere like here, for so long,
in a district general, there's the flow, too,
of starting to belong. My father was a GP,
and although I might not be out in my car
like he was, in people's homes, in doing this
I've still become rooted in the community.

It's the lifeblood of the whole service, I'd say –
relationships. It's those that keep it alive,
and those that would change, too,
if money were allowed to enter the room.

Not just between patients and doctors,
but for the staff as well. I don't know,

we'd all still care, of course, but, well, there'd be
a different reason, wouldn't there? Behind it all.
An altered relationship with the system.
And a knowledge that the nature of our offering –
our time, our skill, our talk even – would be limited
to those who had a certain job or could pay.

I for one, never want to see that day.

> *Another acute case arrives in A&E.*
> *A middle-aged man in motorcycle leathers.*

Giovanni

Each shift is unpredictable, of course it is,
but still, there's always the stuff you can set your clock by –
the fights on a Friday night, the drunks kicking off,
broken bones when there's ice and, pretty much,
any sunny Sunday around 3 p.m., a trauma off a motorbike.

> *PROFESSOR AL-JUBORI, a consultant surgeon,*
> *is scrubbing up for an operation.*

Prof. Al-Jubori

Specialising in obesity, I'm asked that a lot,
about patient responsibility. And yes, of course,
all of us have a duty to reduce risk where we can,
to look after our body.

But at the same time we're here to engage, treat,
not judge, and with something like obesity
it's not as simple as genetics or who overeats.
No, it's a societal disease, and as such we're all involved.

When you dig in it's about inequality, unemployment,
education, public transport, and yes –
and I'm from Iraq, so I understand this – poverty.
In that way, I think, the NHS is useful as a barometer.

It has the cohesion, the scale and reach
to measure and monitor these trends in our culture.
The medical effects of diet, loneliness, drinking or drugs.
And the research, too, to try and tackle them.

It's that, though, I'm most worried about.
The effect of Brexit upon such research, collaboration.
I mean, the NHS, it's the best in the world,
but has become so by embracing other nations,

in its staff, like me and thousands of others,
but also in the way its voice, opinion carries,
to other countries, other doctors.
It leads in so much, but it can't lead alone,

so yes, leaving the EU, in my job,
that's a cause for concern.
Because these diseases of society – obesity, diabetes,
dementia – as we find cures and treatments

for more conventional illnesses,
these are where the strain will come
and so where we really need to be in,
not out, of the global conversation.

>MELISSA *is treating a patient in their home.*

Melissa

It has all got more complex – the patients getting older,
and litigation, that's a growing pressure.

There are different expectations, I guess.
Back when I started, the farmers, they'd bring in eggs

to say thanks. Now with some it's more
a case of 'I deserve this, or I deserve that'.

It's still a privilege, though –
to go into someone's home or to be giving them care

when they've no one else there.
And to be doing it, too, on the NHS. I mean,

most of my patients are poor – in a paying system,
well, a lot would just never present.

>JO, *a district nurse, is in her car, driving to a patient.*

Jo

It is a privilege – to practise what we do

not on a ward or in surgery
but in the intimate space of a home, a family.

A world away from where I began –
in acute medicine. Every day, anything
could come in, and did. Heart attack,

chronic, respiratory. I loved it.
The unpredictable aspect, the adrenaline.
So when I switched to district nursing,

well, I found it hard, that change of pace
and, I suppose, that other switch too –
from never knowing what would come through the door,

to being unsure, instead, of what I'd find
when I knocked on one and entered.
That first visit, though, it's vital –

to assess the risks, the need and, of course,
to start to make that bond. Obviously,
that gets stronger with those you see every day –

the chronic, the diabetic.
One woman, we spent Christmas with her family.
Another man, he put us in his will

because, well, for him, that's what we'd become.
District nursing, though,
it's far from an easy option.

Wouldn't be so hard to recruit if it was.
No, the travelling for one, that's tough,
as is the autonomy. I know, it's a liberty,

but stressful too, especially now
we have to think so much about accountability.
But no doubt, above all, a privilege.

To find someone bedridden, with pressure sores,
and then over a course of visits
see them get better. I mean, is there anything nicer?

> *The motorcyclist has been transferred*
> *to RAV's specialist unit.*
> *As RAV prepares for theatre—*

Rav

What do I give my patients? Well, in essence,
mostly, time. A longer life. But for me, it's more a question
of what I *don't* take from them – that's the greatest gift.

Speech, movement, personality.
Because, let's face it, what I have my hands in here,
is somebody.

That's what we're talking about when I cut into a brain –
a person's character, memory, who they are.
I make a mistake, and the results are immediate.

If it's a success, that's seen further down the line:

a longer life and as much functioning brain
as when they came in. That's the aim.

So yes, it's about damage control.
About taking away the tumour, the contusion,
but also not taking too much.

Because in neurosurgery, you see, we're yet to learn
how to fix, replace. All we can do is remove
and let the brain's plasticity do the rest.

In that way, I suppose, it's somewhat rudimentary.
And yet it never ceases to fascinate me.

By now RAV is operating.

I mean, look at it – the fine mesh of vessels,

these pulsating folds. The closest thing,
some would say, to the human soul.
It is us, and yet all we really know is its structure,

not much else. MRI, CT scans, that's what they show –
the architecture. But how it works? Where memory lives?
No, we know more about the air on Jupiter.

That's what I always think when I see a bruise like this.
Red, swollen, like that planet's crimson eye,
a reminder, every time, of just how far

65

we still have to explore
into the universe of the brain,
the uncharted galaxies of who and how we are.

> *BEN, a consultant psychiatrist, is driving to a home visit*
> *as part of a mental health crisis team.*

Ben

Mental health, it's been there from the start, hasn't it?
In the NHS, I mean. Bevan made a point of it –
insisted it should be part of the service.

Even so, I'd say we still separate it too much
from how we think and treat the physical.
Which is odd, because that's hardly how they exist, is it?

And the aims, the outcomes, they're the same:
making people better, saving lives, keeping them together,
as a person and with each other.

It's just where a surgeon works with a body or a brain
we try to do the same while working with a mind.
Because both, if they're ill, can kill you.

The risk, that's the most exhausting for me –
the judging of it, and the carrying it, too.
Because you can't just admit everyone who's a possibility.

If you did, the wards would be overflowing.
So you have to make a call, assess,

and yes, that does mean some nights I'll go home

worrying if someone will be there tomorrow.
I'll wake up, often, thinking about that. And then the relief!
When you come in the next day and there they are, okay.

Two things, I think, make it even harder.
Firstly, our job is to get to know someone,
and that's why I love it. Them, their family, their stories.

So when you lose them, well, it's just horrible.
You've made that connection. It hits the team hard,
and it always, regardless, feels like our fault,

even when mostly it's not. The other issue is related to that –
the fact that in the eyes of the public,
as an outcome, suicide is never acceptable.

But if you compare this to the rest of medicine, that isn't fair.
I mean, patients under cardiologist care
might die from heart disease, and often do. That's accepted.

But someone under the mental health services?
Who takes their own life? That's not. That's something
gone wrong. And make no mistake,

that's always the first question. What did we miss?
But nine times out of ten, we didn't miss anything.
It was just an outcome, a symptom of their condition.

Andrew

There was no one trigger really,
just a bad run of months. My stepdad,
well, we'd never got on, so soon as he could
he chucked me out of our home.

Then a few weeks later my best friend died.
I just felt empty, alone. I turned to drink
and started self-harming too,
as a way, I suppose, of trying to feel.

I didn't know, see, how to deal with it.
Losing my friend. I ended up on the street,
suicidal. It was the police, in the end,
who put me in touch with the mental health teams.

I was numb to it all back then, that support.
It's crazy really, the last thing you want
is to connect, and yet all around you are these people
doing just that, finding out about you, making a plan:

the psychiatrists in the hospital, then the crisis team
visiting me daily when I had no one else around
in a flat I'd been given by the charity MIND.
They were a lifeline, that team. Made me believe

I deserved to be here. And so good at their jobs –
not that I realised that at the time –

always talking to each other about my best way forward.
But knew, too, when to pull back. Cos it's easy, isn't it?

To become dependent on care, attention, like that.
I can't remember their names but I still see their faces
when I go to dark places, and in that way,
I suppose, they're still helping me now.

They made me see, too, how when things go south
you've got to reach out.
But then that's why I'm so grateful, really.
Cos even if I'd known that before, it only works – doesn't it? –

if there's something there, someone, to reach out for.

Ben

On the whole, though, the good of this job
vastly outweighs the bad.
I'm humbled by the insights I've had

into people's lives, the stories they want to tell,
and the array of patients I've met.
I mean, mental illness, it doesn't care, does it?

About class or social status. It hits everybody.
My colleagues, too, they're extraordinary –
you throw them a name, could be from years ago,

and they'll remember, their histories, their cases.
But then, that's the most rewarding aspect –

being a part of patients' lives. And why I entered

this field. Not just to find out what's wrong
and how to heal them, but also who they are.
If you do that, it's not so much watching them get better

as watching them escape, that's how I think of it.
They're enveloped by a condition, an alter ego,
and with our help the person inside emerges from it.

And even if they don't, there can still be
a positive side. Watching them optimise their situation –
return home, to work, get on with their lives.

> *BEN arrives at a home and knocks on the door.*
> *GWYN answers, carrying his son.*
> *ELUNED is behind him, holding SIRIOL.*

Eluned

It was about two, three days after we brought her home,
a month, I suppose, after she was born.
I couldn't sleep, was pinned to the bed all night,

with anxiety, fear, terrible thoughts.
I knew, then, that something was wrong,
just when it was all meant to be so right.

I went to the GP and asked for help,
and within an hour the crisis team were here,
in our home, giving us care.

Gwyn

It's a concept brought over from Australia.
The idea of keeping a patient at home
in their community, their family,
instead of admitting them –
while still offering the same service
as hospital one-to-one attention.

We'd expected, of course, elements of the system
to follow us here – health visitors, physios,
the regular services after a birth. But this –
it was incredible, humbling to see, and yes,
to receive as well. Because of course Eluned
was the focus, and Siriol, but in effect,
well, they held us all.

And if they hadn't? If the ethos of the NHS
had stopped at those hospital walls?
I don't know what would have happened.
Something worse, for sure.
And I suppose in the past often did,
which, well, just makes you feel lucky, doesn't it?

Bethan

It's getting easier as Eva gets older –
as her problems are crossed off the list.
But then as she does, there's other things too,
that can enter the picture.
Mental health issues, for example,
such as schizophrenia.

That frightens me, of course.
But knowing the NHS is there, the system,
that's a consolation in itself, of sorts.

> *SARA, a geriatrics nurse, is running a bath.*

Sara

It can be hard, when they first come in,
but then put yourself in their shoes.
They'll have already been to A&E, or EAU,
and before that been brought in from a care home, probably.

Imagine, then, how confusing that must be,
when every few minutes you lose your memory?
So yes, they can be agitated, aggressive even,
which is distressing, to see someone that old

being restrained by security.
That's why it's so lovely when they start to settle,
get to know the nurses, calm down.
The memory boxes are amazing for that.

The deputy sister, she makes them up – things from the war,
the 1950s, photos of clothes and period dresses.
It's like time travel then, talking to them,
because, well, those things, they take them there,

so suddenly, back to their lives.
That's when I first got a glimpse
of who we had in those beds.

So much loving and losing, history, experience.

It's why I like the talking – mostly as we wash them,
in the bath or a shower, which is the best time
to bring up the past, and sometimes the present, too.
Find out how they are and what's happening at home.

But yeah, those boxes, they work a treat.
Funny, isn't it? How the thing that gets them
so lost – their memory –
is that which can find them again.

> SAMANTHA *is stacking glasses behind the bar*
> *of a pub she manages.*

Samantha

When you see it first hand, I tell you,
it's crazy how much they have to do,
as well as the general nursing.

Just after my op, one of them told
my mum it was time to go home,
visiting hours were over.

Well, Mum, she blew –
'My daughter's just had a procedure
in which she almost died.
So if you're going to chuck me out
you'll need to get security.'

73

Minutes later and that nurse was back
with a Z-bed, blankets and a cup of tea.
'Don't you worry,' she said, 'you make yourself comfy.'

Valeria

You have to accept, from early on,
that not every patient will like you, and that's fine.
You just have to do whatever is in their best interest.

If you stick to that, you can't go far wrong.
And even if they shout at you, it's usually the system
they're angry with, a procedure being cancelled,

that kind of thing. I just try to explain, calm them.
Once they are, most apologise, either there and then,
or the next time you're in.

Kemi

Yes, the abuse can be difficult.
If you've been up all night and someone's drunk,
having a go at you. I've been pushed, punched.

But you know, most times, at the root of it
is fear, worry, although I do think,
talking to the older doctors,

there's been some change too, in expectation, entitlement.
I worry, if patients ever become customers,
what might happen on that front.

Janice

Eight days later I came back
to a fracture clinic. I'd never seen
so many broken bodies in my life.

Arms, legs, ankles, wrists.
And such a diverse room of people too,
of all ages and backgrounds,

with every plaster holding not just a bone
but a story as well, of that moment when life
took an unexpected turn

and a sudden pain brought them,
with all their different pasts and futures, here,
to be put back together again.

Rav

Yes, you do have to be confident, some would say arrogant,
to operate on such an organ. And yes, it can give you
an ego. I mean, for the families, you're performing the acts of
    a god,

giving them their son, their mother back, creating more life.
But it's made me humble, too. And not just
because it's a privilege, but also through what you see.

So many bolts from the blue. Young lives cut down,
people waking, going about their day,
then stopped in their tracks by a tumour, a stroke,

a crash on a bike. It leaves you thinking, of course it does,
if them why not me or my children, my wife?
Which is why I always say to people,

'Don't postpone.
Who knows what's round the corner?
So live for the here, each other.'

A nurse, ANNIE, is doing observations in the
Coronary Care Unit.

Annie

Often, especially if they're elderly,
we have to be their windows –
I mean, when you're ill, really ill,
your world closes in.

So that's something else we can do,
beyond the general care. Talk, listen.
For many, if they live alone,
that's a treatment in itself.

So yeah, we try to be an opening –
to their past, their lives outside
and, hopefully, to their lives after too,
when they'll leave.
And oh, when they do, that's the best!
When a patient gets well, then comes back . . .

She begins to well up.

76

Sorry,
I'm thinking of a particular gentleman, see,
admitted with pains in his chest,

then went downhill fast. He needed a transplant,
and for a long time it looked like we'd lose him.
But we didn't. He had that new heart
and then came back, to say thank you.

Oh, to see him! Transformed. Only fifties, not old.
So yeah, to see him with all those years before him,
years we'd help give him, wonderful that was.

Steve

I encourage my patients, when they're better,
to go back to critical care, say hello.
Otherwise the nurses there, they only ever see them ill.

Which is, I think, denying them the greatest pleasure.
Seeing that person, who for weeks, maybe, they've cared for,
washed, treated, worried they'd lose,

now out of bed and back in their clothes,
their own life again. I mean, isn't that
why we're all here? To make that happen?

Samantha

If it hadn't been here, then, well,
nor would I be. I mean, my mum,
she had Crohn's disease too,

77

and when she was pregnant they had to operate –
take out her womb. A specialist nurse held it,
with me inside. Kept me alive.

And they have done since, too.
Every six weeks, more or less.
So yeah, held me from the very start, the NHS.

The diagnosis, knowing what I've got,
it's meant everything to me.
My life is, well, a million times better.

I'm setting up an arts centre, in Newport.
Before, there's no way I'd have done that.
And I spend time in Calais too, volunteering.

So just think about it – without my diagnosis,
my treatment, every six weeks,
the people in Newport wouldn't be getting that space,

and the refugees I help, well, I wouldn't be there.
Now multiply that across the whole NHS
and it blows your mind, it really does.

These chains of care, contribution,
all set in motion by a service that's free
and owned by you, me, everybody.

MATTHEW is collecting his grandchildren from school.

Matthew

Working in it all those years, yes,
it did make me, well, a bit more socialist
I suppose, which let me stress

was never my natural position. Still isn't.
But then, how could it not?
When you see the idea in practice

week in, week out, it can't help but affect you.
To operate, in the space of an hour or two,
as I did once, on a lord then a rough sleeper,

to see that equality of care, in front of you
in the theatre, it imbues you with something.
And over time, I think, it made me see

how the NHS, it contributes, maybe,
to more than just the health of the nation.
It's about social cohesion, isn't it?

A shared idea embodied in an entity
that enables our society to discover,
and witness, its humanity.

Valeria

What would I say to him?
Well, mostly thank you, I guess.
And that he must be really proud –
of all the people he's helped.

Melissa

Well, thank you. But then,
it was born of the people, really, wasn't it?
But yeah, thanks, because at the end of the day
it's about life, isn't it?

Giovanni

Congratulations! It's a great invention.
Because, you know, you can really judge
a country's civilisation from how well
the government cares for its people.

Janice

Oh, I don't know. Sorry, that's got me a bit tearful.
Thank you, I suppose. And probably
I'd want to ask him, too,
how should we hold the legacy?

Rav

I'd say well done, it's a fantastic vision,
and yes, the concept is good.
But I'd ask him, too, if he came back,
to appeal to the public about what they want.
Because, you know, we can only deliver
what we put into it.

Kemi

What anyone would, I guess. Thank you.
Because your experiment has been so successful.

Though I'd want to apologise, I think,
on behalf of my generation, too.
Because I'm not so sure we're protecting,
as best we could, its core values.

Bethan

Oh my god. Words wouldn't be enough. Because I mean,
well, without him, Eva, she might not be here, would she?
Or if she was, would have such a different life.

Anvi

Just thank you. For showing a different way,
and having the belief to do it properly.

Rachel

And for the . . . balance, yes, balance
it's put into society.

Vijay

Just admiration, really.
And not just for the culture it's produced
but also the speed with which he made it happen.
So yeah, respect. You're the man!

Prof. Al-Jubori

I would kiss his hands!

Death

before you even saw

Those who live in mountainous countries are
always afraid of avalanches, and they know that
avalanches start with the movement of a very
small stone . . . The pebble starts, but nobody
bothers about the pebble until it gains way, and
soon the whole valley is overwhelmed . . . What
is to be squeezed out next year? Prescriptions?
Hospital charges? Where do you stop? The Health
Service will be like Lavinia - all the limbs
cut off and eventually her tongue cut out, too
. . . The National Health Service was something
of which we were all very proud, and even
the Opposition were beginning to be proud of
it. It only had to last a few more years to
become a part of our traditions, and then the
traditionalists would have claimed the credit
for it all. Why should we throw it away?

— Aneurin Bevan,
resignation speech, 1951

The hospital at night.
HYWEL pushes ALICE along a corridor towards her ward.

Hywel

Well, one thing's for sure.
Bevan did good and so did his idea.
In the years after it all began,
even his most ardent critics
were queuing up to praise it.

Even Willink, Bevan's predecessor,
was generous enough to admit
that 'the Labour government was right
when it undertook the daunting step'
of nationalising the hospitals of the country,
municipal and voluntary.

It was, though, from America
the most exhaustive survey came,
with Dr Lindsay, its author, describing
the new national scheme
as 'magnificent in scope . . . breath taking'.

Yvonne

All well and good – reviews, committees –
but to Bevan the assessment that mattered the most
was that of the people – us.

Ninety-eight per cent of the country
signed up with their local GP.
More than thirty thousand new hospital beds

and drastic cuts in infant mortality rates.
Some of this, of course, was down
to housing, sanitation, new drugs.

But *that*, Bevan said, was exactly the point.
Under the old way such knowledge
would still have been there,

but out of reach for those who most needed the care.
To illustrate this, and the capability
of research in the NHS,

he often turned to the plight of the deaf
and to those who'd received, for free,
over the last ten years,

an NHS device to help them hear.
Five hundred and eighty thousand in total.
And with each hearing aid given

another person taken
from a 'twilight life' of disability
back into the flow of work, society.

The service's 'secret, silent column',
as Bevan liked to call it,

made up of those in the population

who, following treatment,
were now, through their employment,
paying back into the system.

Hywel

Perhaps most telling, though,
in terms of how Bevan viewed the idea's success,
is the story of a single gift.

A handkerchief, silk and crocheted round the edge,
sent to him for Jennie, his wife,
from a Lancashire woman who'd worked all her life,

since the age of twelve, in the cotton mills.
With it, she'd included a letter of thanks
for the dentures and glasses she'd received,

free of charge on the NHS.
The last sentence of her letter read:
'Dear God, reform thy world beginning with me,'

but the words, we're told,
that got to Bevan the most, were these:
'Now,' she wrote, 'I can go into any company.'

There was a strict rule in Bevan's ministry –
any unsolicited presents should be sent straight back.
Which they were, Nye being careful never to accept.

Except, that is, this handkerchief,
which was, along with that letter, in all those years
when he was minister, the only gift he ever kept.

> *HYWEL brings ALICE into her ward.*
> *She is under the care of VIJAY, who, along with a nurse,*
> *begins reviewing her observations.*

> *As HYWEL rolls the empty wheelchair back down*
> *the corridor—*

Hywel

Cradle to grave, that was the concept,
and, god knows, I can vouch for that.
Within an hour, some days,

I'll go from being a stork one moment,
wheeling a newborn onto the ward,
to old Charon the next,

pushing a body, minutes later,
over the river and down to the morgue.
Because, well, we all have our seasons, don't we?

Our sand in the glass. And not just people, either.
Plants, trees, animals, anything that lives.
Like ideas. I don't know,

sometimes you can't help wonder, can you?
Given the direction of travel,

if the sand in this glass isn't, well, running out?

How, though, exactly, might that happen?
How might an idea, once alive, come to die?
I'll tell you. From inside.

Hollowed out, without you noticing,
until it's gone, before you even saw
that it was going.

That's how.

Vijay

It was in my third year,
on rotation at St Mary's, that it first hit me,
just how hard this job could be.

The placement I was on was surgical
and my registrar, he'd worked eight to eleven
straight for, I don't know, six days? Seven?

Making decisions all that time, operating,
keeping patients alive.
He sat us down to do some teaching

and when I looked in his eyes . . .
he was exhausted, worn thin.
He looked about fifty, sixty,

but when I asked later

how old he really was,
they told me – thirty-five.

Then I soon discovered myself,
final year, in clinical,
not just the strain of those shifts

but being, too, so short of staff.
I'd come in when I was ill,
still do – just last Christmas

I worked it all through, six days,
feeling awful with flu.
But if I hadn't, then who . . .?

Junior doctors, see, in a hospital,
they're the engine room.
But you know, that culture that first drew me,

in many ways it gets stronger
when the shit really hits the fan,
when all your backs are to the wall.

It pulls you together, which is still
what I love – how in the NHS staff care
for the patients, but also each other.

That isn't, though, always true.
Other pressures can, well,
cause that culture to fracture.

In that final year, for example,
I was working in England
when the row broke out

with the government, about our contracts.
That was tough. You're exhausted, giving your all,
dealing with life-and-death stuff

like this – trying to assess whether
a patient, if their body stops,
should have resus or not –

while in the press you're
being questioned, misrepresented.
No one I knew wanted to strike,

but we had to. It was about the wellbeing
of patients and the NHS,
about tired doctors not being safe,

making mistakes through lack of sleep.
So yes, we did,
marched on Downing Street.

Kemi

It's odd, isn't it? I mean, it feels as if, in seventy years,
we've done a complete turn, 180 degrees.
At the birth of this it was a minister of health

who had the vision, believed, was inspirational,

and the BMA who were sceptical.
Now, it feels as if it's the other way round

and it's the doctors who are fighting
to save the idea while government,
well, it's almost like they've given up on it,

or want it to break, even though
there'd be an outcry if it went.
I mean, among the public

support for universal health care is at 88 per cent.
But yeah, it's alienated a generation,
all that. Fewer entering for training,

while others are just getting out.
Which is my main concern.
I mean, the NHS *is* the people

who embody the idea, the staff and the patients.
So if you leave them disillusioned,
disheartened, well, what then?

Annie

The hardest part? Being so short-staffed,
that's what I'd say. And that's only getting
worse now, isn't it? I mean,

we've had amazing Spanish nurses here
and Portuguese, Romanian, Italian.

But now, with Brexit, well, they've

either gone or are thinking of going,
while the new trainees from those countries,
they've just stopped applying.

It isn't just the stress all that brings,
the lack of attention you can pay,
but also what it does to the way that we work.

When you get over-stretched
and when there are cuts,
it becomes territorial, everyone looking out

for their own department,
until, instead of collaboration,
you're thinking more in terms of protection.

So yeah, it does get frustrating,
when everyone's working so hard,
above and beyond,

to see so many bad stories in the press
about the NHS. Especially when, in terms
of patient experience, it's overwhelmingly positive.

I mean, think how many people it treats every day
who have no reason to complain.
But those stories, well, they don't make headlines, do they?

Steve

Nor does the fact it's been judged, again and again,
as among the best in the world, for quality, access, efficiency.
And that's with us spending the least on health
of all the G7 countries.

Which is why that weight of negative press
is so dangerous. In terms of the public, I think,
it can make them forget – just how good it is,
and what we have. It's sowing the seeds of doubt, isn't it?

Making it a battle of stories. And where will that lead?
I mean, this whole system was partly built on belief,
shared purpose, and it's *that* which keeps it afloat.
You erode the idea, then people start to think,

'Actually, this is impossible, we're asking too much.'
The whole 'bottomless pit' argument, when really it's not.
A world-class service needs a world-class budget,
simple as that. Underfund it, then yes, at times,

you'll make the broken story true – winter pressures,
    outbreaks of flu.
But there's a difference, isn't there? Between breaking
under pressure and the system being broken.
The idea behind it – I'd say that's still intact,

doesn't need to be changed or reformed to fit us.
More, in fact, it's *us* who should raise our game to meet it.

I don't know. You hear people saying
we need to find another way, which is madness –

because we found one already, seventy years ago,
and it worked, too, better than imagined,
which is why when they saw it other countries
wanted to follow. Yes, it'll always need to flex, reform,

just as Bevan said it should. But the ethos at its heart?
You take that away – start implanting private providers,
marketisation, companies who'll answer
not to the patient but the shareholder –

do this, and you change the very nature
of the belief behind the care,
the unique, life-giving rhythm that's kept it going,
that's made it what it is, and us who we are.

Annie

Then added to those stories in the press,
there's all the other kinds of pressure.
Pay freezes, nurses losing their bursaries,
cuts in social services.

I don't know, sometimes it seems
it's like they want us to break.
But then you stop and think, surely
they can't want that?

LEANNE, a maxillofacial surgeon,
is studying a computer-generated reconstruction
of the motorcyclist's face.

Leanne

Here, in maxillofacial, we deal with everything
above the neck – broken jaws, malunion, cleft palate,
eyes, oral. Which means the physical trauma
or conditions we see are also an injury to identity.

Our human face, our speech, our expression –
it's who we are in the world, our interface for empathy.
So you can imagine the damage that can be done
when it's these that need, but are also affected by, our surgery.

My scalpel isn't just cutting or reconstructing
bone, skin, but also, in many ways, someone's psychology.
It means I'm more cautious, perhaps, than other surgeons,
in terms of making a patient aware of the risks.

But the rewards, too, can be so much richer.
A face renewed, speech returned, but also something deeper.
The other aspect I love is being involved in not just removal,
but growth, too – the body's talent for knowing what to do.

Take tongue cancer, for example. With that
we'll often remove half of it – the tongue, I mean –
then harvest some skin from the wrist, with a vein attached.
That, in turn, we sew into a facial artery,

moulding the skin into the existing tongue. And what happens?
Because it's inside the mouth that wrist skin responds –
becomes oral mucosa, adapts to its environment.
The body takes over, heals itself essentially.

Which is what a healthy system does, I suppose,
if it's allowed to be.

KERRY is in her office looking out at the maternity garden.

Kerry

It's become so important, this garden.
For the parents and for me.
And not just for right after it's happened, either,
when they come in to recover, hang something on the tree.

No, for long after, too. I always tell them,
'Come back, anytime. No need for an appointment.'
And they do. On the anniversary, of course, with family,
but at other times too, to plant something or just be alone.

I'll give them a wave if I see them, out the window.
I don't know, I suppose for me it's about
letting them know they're not on their own.

*WENDY is on the maternity ward,
caring for new and expectant mothers.*

Wendy

I love my job and don't know a midwife who doesn't.

But at the same time, would I recommend it?
Just last week my niece, she said she was going to train as one.
'You shouldn't,' that's what I told her.

Why? The stress, mostly, of too few staff, litigation.
When I trained I was warned, it's not if but when
in terms of being sued. That can get to you.
I know of several midwives, and good ones too,

who are working the tills of Waitrose now, instead.
Just couldn't take the pressure, the strain.
I'm a single mum and when my kids were still young
I had to work nights, it was the only way.

Used to put them to bed, then come in and work a full shift,
getting back just in time to wake them,
make them breakfast, get them to school.
An hour of housework, then I'd sleep, 'til they came home.

Kemi

It's overused as a phrase but it's true,
I wanted to train as a doctor 'to help people',
and not just with their quality of life either,
but the quality of their death, too.

It's become one of the things
I'm proudest about, in the NHS,
how, when it's done right, we now collaborate
with a patient and relatives rather than dictate.

If that goes well, then really you treat
everyone, the patient but also the family,
the collective memory.
And if there is no family, well then,

you've had the privilege of providing dignity, comfort,
in the most intimate of moments.
The other reason I chose medicine, though,
like many of us, was the NHS itself.

What it stands for, what it says about us.
So yes, I am nervous, like lots of my generation,
that we may witness, while we work in it,
the service's dissolution, as it becomes more commercial,

and the changes that would bring to everything –
the doctor–patient relationship, the purchase of drugs,
the ethos of being a team, access, and yes, for me,
despite the stress, the very reason I still come in.

That's why I joined the strike, for the NHS
and patient wellbeing. And why, too,
we've been discussing, recently in the BMA,
a motion to propose the whole system

is shifted out of the political orbit
and away from parties and government,
so this idea, made manifest by politics,
can survive beyond the reach of Parliament.

Karen

It started in 1990, when they introduced
the internal market, the purchaser–provider split,
after which hospitals were meant to compete.
Admin costs soared soon after that.

Then came the public–private partnerships,
companies providing elective services,
diagnostic tests, cataracts, knees, hips, that kind of thing.
All under the NHS logo, of course,

like some kind of Kitemark, I suppose.
Anyway, on average, for every patient they saw,
compared to the NHS, they were paid
12 per cent more – as a sweetener –

and were paid in bulk too, so still got
the money if the procedures happened or not.
That all cost a lot – over the first five years, 5.6 billion,
with the NHS still picking up the tab

for any legal or clinical complication.
But that was nothing to PFI – Private Finance Initiatives,
created to build and run infrastructure projects.
Hospitals made up the most of those,

but again, at a massive cost. The repayments,
you see – like a mortgage – are huge and at rates
sometimes as much as 70 per cent.
They put many hospitals in dire straits,

forcing mergers, bed reductions, service closures.
The total bill for all projects, after capital worth,
stands at around 240 billion. Now, imagine,
what could the NHS do with that?

I'll tell you what – run, for two years, its entire budget.
Look, I'm a GP. I treat, diagnose
but if the NHS were my patient,
it would seem clear enough to me.

When costs are driven by profit incentive
not medical need, well,
then the companies brought in to heal,
tend to create, instead, a traumatic bleed.

Samantha

If it went? Well, personally, I'd die,
simple as that. Without treatment
the life expectancy for someone like me,

with Crohn's disease, would be around fifty.
So what would that give me? Five, ten more years?
Every six weeks I come here,

see the same nurse who weighs me, takes my blood,
then hooks me up to an IV. Six thousand quid,
that's how much each session costs.

Imagine, then, me trying to get insured
with a chronic condition like that?

I can't even get cover to travel abroad.

More generally, I think it would show
we've forgotten how to care. Who we are.
We'd have lost whatever it was we won after the war –

I mean, in terms of community.
Back then a bomb could hit anyone's home, couldn't it?
And I reckon that was a leveller –

everyone in the same kind of danger.
But when you think about it, it should be the same,
shouldn't it? With cancer, illness.

Because like those bombs they don't discriminate,
do they? Nor, then, should the health care
to fight them, that's what I say.

Vijay

That pain I spoke about earlier?
The kind that folds you in,
locks you in the present moment only.
That, from what I've seen,
is the kind of pain this system is in.

Which is so frustrating, because you know
there are reforms to be made,
and can be too, not from outside, either,
but from within.

For something the size of the NHS,
it's surprisingly efficient – one of the best –
but I'd say we could be better again
if only we had the time, the space,
to take it in hand. But how can you?

If you're always in that present moment of pain?
When underfunding, staff shortages,
mean you're in a constant position
of defence, crisis?

Sometimes I wish we could turn the whole thing
off and then back on again.
And not just to give us that time
but also as a way to prove it –
the preciousness of what we have,
through the grief we'd feel in losing it.

I've seen that happen with patients, relatives,
so often. The value of a person
only truly felt when they're gone.
I know we can't do that, but imagine if we did,
and for that year the public had to live
under a private or insurance-based system?

Maybe, then, they'd fight for it more.
Because I think they'll have to, if it's going to survive.
At the moment we are, the doctors, from the inside,
but at the end of the day it's the people's service,
and so with them the power lies to save it.

Alison

This was back in August.
We had a young girl come in with cerebral palsy –
had a nasty sepsis. Lovely girl, almost twenty.

When I looked at her birthday I saw,
she was only a month younger
than my eldest daughter. Anyway,

she'd never spoken, nor been mobile,
but she could communicate, in a way,
with her mam. All this, you see,

is the kind of thing taken into consideration.
Because it was clear she wouldn't make it,
that the only treatment now was palliation.

In light of that her mother and father
asked if they could take her home, to die.
Well, we weren't sure what to say –

it would mean a portable ventilator
and a nurse, too, to remove the tube
there, in the home. But it could be done,

so my manager, she said to me,
'Will you be the one? The nurse who'll

accompany them?' So I did.

We took her home, helped the parents
get her up to her bedroom, then they left
while I got her dressed, into some pyjamas, her own.

It was, if I'm honest, lovely –
to see her there, surrounded by photos,
her own bedclothes, her chair.

Everything that was part of her being her.
When I was done I called the family back in,
said, 'Look, I'm going to have a coffee,

so when you're ready, let me know
and I'll come and remove that ventilator tube.'
Just the day before I'd had a conversation on the phone,

with a woman from some office.
'Do you feel qualified for this?' she'd asked.
'You'll be on your own, without your unit, support.

Anything goes wrong you'll be held to account.'
'I'm taking a girl to her home to die,' I said.
'With her family. What more support could I want?'

Not to say I wasn't nervous, I was.
But you know, in the end, the happening of it
was all the answer I needed.

After fifteen minutes they called me back in.
I removed the tube and some hours later,
she died. But in that time in between,

well, so many people came to see her,
be with her, and with her mam
holding her hand all the way through.

Not on a ward, mind, or on a hospital unit,
but there, where she belonged,
in her daughter's bedroom.

It felt like a gift, and yes, I suppose
it was. But for me things like this,
it's in the DNA of the NHS,

to be able to give like that;
to offer more, not less, to its patients,
who are, after all, the people who own it.

> *GIOVANNI, in A&E, is coming out of the family room.*
> *The relatives of the six-year-old boy are inside,*
> *distraught with grief.*
> *VALERIA is also in the room, comforting them.*

Giovanni

The pain that terrifies me the most is emotional.
With physical pain there's nearly always
a solution – from distraction for children,
to painkillers and opiates.

But for the person who's lost a son or a daughter,
that's when you learn, as a doctor,
what pain really is. Pain that can't be touched
by anaesthetics.

Valeria

I'd been a fully qualified nurse
for about a month by then, so yeah, maybe I'd been lucky.
It had been hard – the long shifts, the new responsibility –
but I'd held it together.

Being assigned to a bereaved family, though,
staying with them all through the night into the day –
it was that which first broke me.
I know we're trained not to get too bonded,

but how can't you? Seeing whole lives, memories,
spreading out from that room.
So much love in distress. And, yeah, I guess,
that's something I'd never really appreciated

about the NHS. When you work in it, day in day out,
you come to see it as a vessel of sorts,
a vessel of all this love – in the relatives' concern,
their care, joy and yes, their grief as well.

You start to really see what people mean to each other,
who we are and how our care can keep them together.
That's what I've come to learn. That this huge machine,
this system, bigger than any other, is still, well, so human.

So yeah, you do get attached, course you do.
Sometimes I'll even phone in, when I'm off,
just to see how someone's doing, or, and this is the worst,
I'll lie in bed after a twelve-hour shift, still thinking about
    them –

did I change that drip, do such and such right?
Because you're always so rushed, aren't you?
All the time – and I guess that's my greatest fear,
getting something wrong, not because I didn't know

what to do, or made a bad choice, but because
I was just too tired, or didn't have the time to give proper care.
It goes the other way too, though – I mean,
sometimes, after a really good day,

I'll get home, and as I'm making my dinner
I'll look at my hands, not quite believing
what, over the last few hours, they've done.
How many people they've washed, treated, comforted.

And what that might mean as well,
to the people for whom those patients
aren't patients at all, but rather
a mother, a brother, a daughter, a son.

The early hours of the morning.

*KEMI has taken over from VIJAY
and is at the bedside of ALICE, assessing her treatment.*

ALICE is unconscious and breathing with difficulty.
KEMI goes to the ward sister's office and makes a phone call.

MATTHEW is travelling to the hospital in a taxi.

Matthew

Real pain, in my experience,
the kind that makes you cry,
is psychological.

Certainly, that's been true for me
and, I'd say, with regard to the NHS,
the pain that worries me the most,

not the physical. That can be fixed.
Better and more investment, stop Brexit,
increased capacity, less party politics,

an increase in nurses' and social care salaries.
But the psychological aspect,
the philosophical even,

once that's broken, well . . .
I mean, I can tell you how to heal
a fracture in a bone.

But a fracture to a soul? That's harder.
I suppose I could compare it, too,
to what I once did: surgery on the brain.

The more you interfere and take away,
the greater the risk to function,
someone remaining who they are.

The same could be said, you see,
of some of the reforms that have been made.
You take away too much of the original idea,

and you alter the personality.
That's not to say changes shouldn't happen,
of course they should – the service

should flex, adapt, to our needs.
Today, that means the elderly, obesity, dementia.
But you know, it isn't

as if we haven't been here before.
Christ, the whole thing came into being overnight,
and right after a war.

And then, just a year or two later,
when its very creation revealed
such depths of health deprivation,

its running costs soared.
But we met that challenge, and rightly too –
I mean, all that meant

was the health needs of the nation,
at last, were being met.

So, if we can do that then,

I'm sure, with the right political will,
we'll be able to do it again.
I certainly hope so, because god knows

I don't want my grandchildren
to be the generation
who'll see those bills on the table again.

> ALICE, *lying in her hospital bed,*
> *speaks from an earlier time.*

Alice

Am I scared? Yes, a little. But you know,
pain does a lot in dispelling a fear of death.
And also, for me, it's not so much a fear of what's next
but rather what I'll be leaving behind.

Lying here, having time to think, you see,
it really does come clear how it's the chain
that's the meaning, that matters. Not so much
the passing away but rather the passing on.

My father, he used to tell me
how he and my mother, they chose to call me Alice
because of Wonderland, and the idea
that the moment I was born, I was there.

Because to them, it was here. Life.

And of course they were right. All capacity for wonder,
and its opposite – ingratitude, expectation –
well, they all reside in us. And this, the NHS,

to create such a monument to the communal,
yet able to care for the individual, well,
it's one of the most wondrous things we've done.
So, thinking about all that, the chain, what I fear is this:

being one of the generations who, having inherited
this beautiful solution, will stop seeing its wonder,
until it becomes so diluted, well, it's gone.
Yes, it's that I don't want – to pass on an age of squander.

No, my grandchildren and everyone else's,
they deserve something better.
I don't know, I suppose it's as simple, really,
as wanting to leave more light in your wake, than shadow.

In the maternity suite a woman goes into emergency labour.
She is attended to by ANVI, WENDY.

MATTHEW arrives at the hospital. He is taken
to ALICE's bedside.
KEMI is already there, along with RAV,
MATTHEW's grandchildren and daughter,
all come to say goodbye to ALICE.

KEMI and MATTHEW have a brief conversation.
KEMI agrees to MATTHEW's request.

KEMI, RAV and the other family members leave the room.
MATTHEW, left alone, lies down beside his wife, ALICE.

In the maternity suite, the baby is born but has no pulse.
The paediatricians rush to resuscitate it.

Out in the corridor HYWEL and YVONNE watch the
sun rise over the hills.

ALICE, with MATTHEW lying beside her,
exhales for the last time.

In the maternity suite, the newborn breathes its first breath
and cries out to the world.

Acknowledgements

The characters and speeches in this book are informed
by over seventy hours of interviews, so I am especially
grateful to the NHS staff and patients who shared their
time, thoughts and memories – without their contributions
this book would not exist in the way it does. I would like to
thank James Hodgson and the Aneurin Bevan University
Health Board communications team for arranging access to
the buildings and staff of Nevill Hall Hospital, and Tracey
Newell, Amy Quant and Joe Williams for their help with the
interviewing process.

I would also like to thank the authors of the following
books and websites, all of which provided invaluable insights
into the founding of the NHS and the nature of its service
today: *Aneurin Bevan* by Michael Foot, *Nye* by Nicklaus
Thomas-Symonds, *Your Life in My Hands* by Dr Rachel
Clarke, *Aneurin Bevan on the National Health Service* edited
by Charles Webster, *How to Dismantle the NHS in Ten Easy
Steps* by Dr Youssef El-Gingihy, www.kingsfund.org.uk.

Mitzi Angel and her team at Faber have had to work at
double speed to ensure this text is published to coincide with
the 70th anniversary of the NHS. Thanks to all, and to my
agents Jane Villers and Zoe Waldie.

To Provide All People was originally commissioned by BBC
Wales and developed as a film-poem with Vox Pictures. I am

grateful to Nick Andrews for enabling us to explore the idea, Adrian Bate for marshalling it through to completion and Pip Broughton for being at my side every step of the way.

Katherine, diolch o galon cariad – *Llawn yw'r coed o ddail a blode, Llawn o gariad merch wyf inne.*

My most heartfelt thanks goes to the staff of the NHS, who every day keep one of our best and most beautiful ideas alive.

The Aneurin Bevan University Health Board, like many Health Boards, has its own charity to supplement its funding. If you would like to donate to this charity, or to any of the other Health Board charities, then please do.

www.wales.nhs.uk/sitesplus/866/page/52338

PINK MIST

Winner of the Hay Festival Poetry Medal, the Wales Book of the Year, and shortlisted for the BBC Audio Drama Awards

Pink Mist is a verse-drama about three young soldiers from Bristol who are deployed to Afghanistan. School friends still in their teens, Arthur, Hads and Taff each have their own reasons for enlisting. Within a short space of time they return to the women in their lives – a mother, a wife, a girlfriend – all of whom must now share the psychological and physical aftershocks of their service.

Drawing upon interviews with soldiers and their families, *Pink Mist* illuminates the effects of the devastating conflict in Afghanistan and the human cost of modern warfare.

'A tremendous book. It feels huge, engulfing, devastating.' *Observer* Poetry Book of the Month

'The war poet of our generation.' *Independent*

'Phenomenal . . . Relevant, riveting British writing . . . Timeless in its depiction of the pity of war . . . Extremely moving.' *Esquire* Book of the Week

www.faber.co.uk

ff

Also by Owen Sheers

THE GREEN HOLLOW

In 1966 a coal-mine waste tip collapsed on a school and surrounding houses in Aberfan, South Wales, killing 144 people, most of them children. Fifty years later Owen Sheers interviewed survivors, parents and rescuers to create a dramatic poem in the voice of the village, then and now. The resulting work is a striking lyrical meditation on belonging, grief and community, fuelled by the loves and losses of those who suffered a tragedy that shouldn't have happened.

Originally created as a BAFTA-winning BBC drama, *The Green Hollow* is a historical story with a deeply urgent contemporary resonance; the story of a community run by a corporation and the shadows cast when a system fails those in its care. It is also, however, a moving poetic portrait of recovery, resistance and renewal, both personal and communal, and a beautiful rendering of memory and lived experience, to commemorate and tribute.

'Aberfan seems to have been left unmarked by any British poet laureate . . . Fifty years on, Owen Sheers has finally offered the tribute due from a laureate.' *Arts Desk*

ff

I SAW A MAN

After the sudden loss of his wife, Michael Turner moves to London to start again. Living in a quiet street in Hampstead, he develops a close bond with the Nelson family next door: Josh, Samantha and their two young daughters.

The friendship at first seems to offer the prospect of healing, but then a devastating event changes all their lives, and Michael finds himself bearing the burden of grief and a terrible secret.

'A tense, intelligent page-turner.' *The Times*

'Quite simply the most stylish thriller I've read: always intelligent, beautifully made, exhilaratingly economical.' *TLS* Books of the Year

'Taut as a thriller, but resonant with motifs of intimacy and distance, guilt and redemption.' *Guardian*

www.faber.co.uk